Pentabus and Theatre by the Lake present

JACARANDA

by Lorna French

CW01080671

‖SAMUEL FRENCH‖

The moral right of Lorna French to be identified as author of this work has been asserted in accordance with Section 77 of the Copyright, Designs and Patents Act 1988.

USE OF COPYRIGHTED MUSIC

A licence issued by Concord Theatricals to perform this play does not include permission to use the incidental music specified in this publication. In the United Kingdom: Where the place of performance is already licensed by the PERFORMING RIGHT SOCIETY (PRS) a return of the music used must be made to them. If the place of performance is not so licensed then application should be made to PRS for Music (www.prsformusic.com.). A separate and additional licence from PHONOGRAPHIC PERFORMANCE LTD.(www. ppluk.com) may be needed whenever commercial recordings are used. Outside the United Kingdom: Please contact the appropriate music licensing authority in your territory for the rights to any incidental music.

USE OF COPYRIGHTED THIRD-PARTY MATERIALS

Licensees are solely responsible for obtaining formal written permission from copyright owners to use copyrighted third-party materials (e.g., artworks, logos) in the performance of this play and are strongly cautioned to do so. If no such permission is obtained by the licensee, then the licensee must use only original materials that the licensee owns and controls. Licensees are solely responsible and liable for clearances of all third-party copyrighted materials, and shall indemnify the copyright owners of the play(s) and their licensing agent, Concord Theatricals Ltd., against any costs, expenses, losses and liabilities arising from the use of such copyrighted third-party materials by licensees.

IMPORTANT BILLING AND CREDIT REQUIREMENTS

If you have obtained performance rights to this title, please refer to your licensing agreement for important billing and credit requirements.

JACARANDA was commissioned by Pentabus. It was first performed at Pentabus Theatre, Bromfield, Shropshire on Thursday 7 October, 2021. The cast was as follows:

OLIVIA DUDZAI . . . . Mara Allen
MATTY TAYLOR . . . . Stuart Laing

Director	Elle While
Designer	Charlie Cridlan
Lighting Designer	Tim Mascall
Sound Designer	Harry Linden Johnson
Puppetry Director	Marie Fortune
Puppetry Direction & Maker	Jo Lakin
Assistant Director	Garen Abel Unokan
Engagement & Audience Development	Melina Morris
Technical Advisor	Benjamin Leonides-Morgan
Production Manager	Fiona Hilton
Stage Manager	Niamh Percy
Casting Consultant	Karishma Balani

With Special Thanks to: Aston Shoot, Virginie Assal – member of Black Girls Hike, Matthew Bulgo, Ilene Chigwende, Jennifer Chigwende, Chinasa Vivian Ezugha, Rhiane Fatinikun – founder of Black Girls Hike, Charlyne Francis, Ignatios Gangaidzo, Juliet Gilkes Romero, Nell Scarlett Goddard Banks, Sarah Goddard, Mat Grenyer, Clare and John Hilton, Dr Olalekan Lee Aiyegbusi, Kevin McCurdy, Sophie Motley, Ginny Schiller.

And special thanks to the Garrick Charitable Trust, who have supported Assistant Director Garen Abel Unokan.

TOUR DATES

Thursday 7 October | Pentabus Theatre, Bromfield | Shropshire
Friday 8 October | Pentabus Theatre, Bromfield | Shropshire
Saturday 9 October | Quatt Village Hall | Shropshire

Friday 15 October | Clungunford Village Hall | Shropshire
Saturday 16 October | SpArC Theatre, Bishops Castle | Shropshire

Thursday 21 October | Leintwardine Centre | Herefordshire
Friday 22 October | Habberley Village Hall | Shropshire
Saturday 23 October | Brilley Village Hall | Herefordshre

Wednesday 27 October | Ropsley Village Hall | Lincolnshire
Thursday 28 October | All Saints' Church, Bradbourne | Derbyshire

Thursday 4 – Saturday 13 November | Theatre by the Lake | Cumbria

Tuesday 16 November | Stephen Joseph Theatre | Yorkshire
Friday 19 November | Skirwith Village Hall | Cumbria
Saturday 20 November | Barningham Village Hall | County Durham
Sunday 21 November | Kirkby Stephen Sports & Social Club | Cumbria

Wednesday 24 November | The Courthouse, Thirsk | Yorkshire

CAST AND CREATIVE TEAM

MARA ALLEN | OLIVIA

Mara graduated from RADA in 2019.

Theatre credits include: *The Night Watch* (The Original Theatre); *Macbeth* (Shakespeare's Globe); *Henry V* (The Maltings Arts Theatre); *A Midsummer Night's Dream* (The Changeling Theatre Company).

STUART LAING | MATTY

Stuart trained at Drama Centre London.

Theatre credits include: *Macbeth* (Chichester Festival Theatre); *The Curious Incident of the Dog in the Night-time* (National Theatre); *Macbeth* (Mercury Colchester); *Peckham: the Soap Opera* (Royal Court); *Miniaturists* (Arcola); *The Furies / Land of the Dead* (UK tour); *The Doll's House* (Belgrade Coventry); *Hundreds and Thousands, Billy and the Crab Lady, Food for Thought, The Games Room* (Soho Theatre); *Blowing Whistles* (Leicester Square Theatre); *Love and Money* (RADA Festival); *Drowning on Dry Land* (Salisbury Playhouse); *Season's Greetings* (Liverpool Playhouse); *A Streetcar Named Desire* (Theatre Clwyd); *Indian Country* (Traverse); *Hushabye Mountain* (Hampstead); *Trouble with Girls* (National Theatre Studio); *Kiss of the Spiderwoman, Over Here* (Leicester Haymarket); *Bad Company* (The Bush) and *Loot* (The Thorndike).

Television credits include: *Vera, Emmerdale, Silent Witness, Father Brown, Trial and Retribution, Casualty, Eastenders, Doctors, The Bill, The Animator, Inspector Lynley Mysteries, Vincent, Wire in the Blood, Francis Tuesday, Spooks, Holby City, Sex and Lies, Poirot: Sad Cypress, Everytime You Look at Me, Murphy's Law, Cambridge Spies, Burn it, Stag, Bob Martin, In a Land of Plenty, In Between, The Listener, Berkeley Square, Heartbeat, How TV Ruined my Life, Love Bites – In Your Dreams, Kavanagh QC, Strikeforce, Blood and Peaches, Devils Advocate, Minder.*

Film credits include: *South West Nine, The Lawless Heart, Butterfly Man, The Great Ecstasy of Robert Carmichael, Lie Still, The Truth Game, Gaston's War, Strong Language, Three Steps to Heaven.*

LORNA FRENCH | WRITER

Lorna French is a playwright, writing workshop leader and dramaturg. Lorna is currently under commission to Limbik Theatre and the *Hear Me Now* monologue series (via Titilola Dawudu and Tamasha Theatre Company). Her most recent writing work includes the short play *I See You Now*, produced as part of the *15 Heroines* plays at Jermyn Street Theatre in November 2020. Also the short radio drama NFA for Menagerie Theatre Company and the University of Cambridge in October 2020.

Esther, a play about Black African Caribbean women of Birmingham and the West Midlands, was inspired by oral history interviews with several local women. It was shortlisted for the Theatre Uncut Political Playwriting Award 2020 and longlisted for the Women's Prize for Playwriting 2020. *Esther* received a staged reading at Midlands Arts Centre (MAC) in 2019 made possible by a Developing Your Creative Practice award from Arts Council England. Other past work includes *The Last Flag*, a co-written Afternoon Drama for BBC Radio 4 and Eclipse Theatre Company in 2018 and a co-written adaptation of *Jane Eyre* for Bolton Octagon, also in 2018. In 2017, Lorna wrote a one-act play called *Transitions* for Birmingham Rep Education Department and RSA Academy. In 2016, she wrote an audio drama called *You Say* for the *White Open Spaces* monologues co-commissioned by Eclipse and Pentabus Theatre. Lorna is a two-time winner of the Alfred Fagon Award (in 2006 and 2016) and has presented work at, or written work for, Birmingham Rep, Oval House, MAC, Young Vic and New Wolsey Theatre.

Lorna is also a lecturer at ICT Manchester and has previously worked as an Associate Lecturer on the Writing for Performance MA and other BA Performing Arts Undergraduate programmes at the University of Derby. She has most recently worked as a dramaturg on *Close to the Edge* by Viv Manjaro (Planet Arts and Red Earth Collective) and on *Revealed* by Daniel Anderson (Rites of Passage Productions).

ELLE WHILE | DIRECTOR

Elle is the Artistic Director of Pentabus Theatre and an Associate Artist at Shakespeare's Globe, where she directed *The Merry Wives of Windsor*, *As You Like It* and *Hamlet*. Her most recent directing work includes *Idyll* for Pentabus, *Private Peaceful* for Nottingham Playhouse and *Blue Stockings* at Storyhouse, Chester. She developed and directed the award-winning production of *Glory Dazed*, which played at Edinburgh and Adelaide festivals before transferring to the Soho Theatre. She was also the revival director for the West End production (Gielgud 2015-17), UK and international tour of the award-winning production, *The Curious Incident of the Dog in the Night-Time*. She has worked prolifically as an associate and assistant director with directors including Lucy Bailey, Marianne Elliott, Nancy Meckler, Ian Rickson, Thea Sharrock and Alex Timbers in the West End and at the RSC, The Old Vic, the National Theatre and the Young Vic.

CHARLIE CRIDLAN | DESIGNER

Theatre credits include: *Christmas at the (Snow) Globe, Merry Wives of Windsor* (Shakespeare's Globe); *We Are Arrested* (RSC & Arcola Theatre); *Day of the Living* (RSC); *Mr Stink* (UK tour & West End); *Shore* (Riverside Hammersmith); *Brixton Stories* (Lyric Hammersmith); *Lights Out Land Girls, Eddie & the Gold Tops* (Bad Apple Theatre); *Parkway Dreams, Getting Here* and *Cuckoo Teapot* (Eastern Angles); *Fury, Detroit* (GSMSD); *Caravan* (Audience Choice Award 2018, Vaults

Festival), *Da Native, Orator* (pick of the week & Audience Choice Award, The Vaults); *Umbra* (Dance Adventures); *Zones* and *Zero For the Young Dudes* (Soho Theatre); *Imogen* (UK tour); *Grimm's Tales, The Labyrinth* (Oval House); *Woody Allen's Murder Mysteries* (Warehouse Theatre); *Christmas Claytime* (Indefinite Articles, Discover Children's Centre).

Opera credits include: *The Pearl Fishers, La Boheme, Carmen, Jago, Eleanor Vale* (Wedmore Opera); *The Magic Flute* (Peacock Theatre); *Wagner Dream* (Barbican Hall).

Site-specific productions include: *Titania's Dream*, Creative Direction / Design (Fulham Palace Gardens); *Herstory* (Arch 468 at Brighton Festival); *Uncle Vanya* (Wilton's Music Hall); *Top Dog Live!* (The Roundhouse); *The Oresteia Trilogy, Don Juan, Toad of Toad Hall, Around the World in 80 Days, The Mother* (Scoop @ More London); *Streets* (Theatre Royal Stratford East, Roof East & Stratford Circus).

TIM MASCALL | LIGHTING DESIGNER
Tim works across theatre, opera and dance and has designed extensively in the West End, across the UK and internationally. Theatre companies he has designed for include: National Theatre of Scotland, Royal Lyceum, Edinburgh, Dundee Rep, Complicite, Theatre Royal Bath, Theatr Clwyd, Menier Chocolate Factory, Rose Theatre Kingston and many others.

Opera credits include: *The Cunning Little Vixen* (Garsington Opera); *Aida* (Opera Holland Park); *Peter Grimes, The Gamblers* (Royal Festival Hall).

HARRY LINDEN JOHNSON | SOUND DESIGNER
Theatre includes: *God of Carnage* (Bath Theatre Royal); *World's End* (King's Head Theatre); *Parakeet* (Paines Plough, Roundabout); *Br'er Cotton* (Theatre 503); *Romeo and Juliet, Richard III* (York Rose Theatre); *Babette's Feast* (Print Rooms Coronet).

As Associate: *Anatomy of a Suicide* (Deutsches Schauspielhaus); *Orlando* (Schaubühne); *Norma Jeane Baker of Troy* (The Shed); *Home I'm Darling* (National Theatre/ Duke of York's) and *Nine Night* (Trafalgar Studios).

MARIE FORTUNE | PUPPETRY DIRECTOR
Marie is a puppetry director, director, puppeteer, actor and co-artistic director of award-winning theatre company Foan & Fortune.

Puppetry directing credits include: *The Hunting of the Snark* (Latitude Festival and UK tour); *Caliban and the Magicke Booke* (British Library / Dubai Arts Theatre); *Mess!* (Little Angel Theatre / Mimetic Festival).

Puppetry directing for film includes: *Little Mess!* (Foan & Fortune / Little Angel Theatre / Attenborough Arts Centre).

JO LAKIN | PUPPETRY DIRECTION & MAKER

Jo is a puppet designer, maker, director and puppeteer. She works across stage and screen for UK and international productions. Jo trained at the Curious School of Puppetry, and is a graduate of the Royal Welsh College of Music and Drama where she was awarded the Phillip and Christine Carne Prize for Theatre Design, and the Paul Kimpton Prize for Innovation.

Puppetry directing and maker credits include: *As You Like It* (Shakespeare's Globe).

Puppetry design and maker credits include: *Christmas Carol A Fairytale* (Wilton's Music Hall); *The Lion, the Witch and the Wardrobe* (Birmingham Repertory Theatre); *How to Hide an Elephant and Circus 1903* (Significant Object); *The Four Seasons* (Gyre and Gimble) and *Crow* (Handspring UK).

Puppet supervisor credits include: *The Wizard of Oz* and *101 Dalmatians* (Birmingham Repertory Theatre).

GAREN ABEL UNOKAN | ASSISTANT DIRECTOR

A writer and director born and bred in South London, now Edinburgh-based, Garen Abel Unokan's previous theatre credits include: *Blend. Share.Mix* (Theatre503); *Glutathione* (Young Vic) and *Can I Touch Your Hair?* (Vault Festival).

In 2018, she was the Young Vic's Boris Karloff Trainee Assistant Director, supported by the Boris Karloff Foundation on *The Convert* by Danai Gurira and directed by Ola Ince. Her writing has appeared in publications such as *The New Yorker* and *Black Ballad*, and she is currently working on her debut novel. As an artist, Garen is particularly interested in narratives surrounding queerness, blackness, coming of age, grief and families – whatever shape they take.

PENTABUS

Pentabus is the nation's rural theatre company. We are the only professional theatre company in the UK whose vision is singularly rural. We tour new plays about the contemporary rural world to new audiences in village halls, fields, festivals and theatres, telling stories with local relevance, plus national and international impact. We believe that every person living in an isolated rural community has a right to exceptional theatre. We are based in a Victorian school in rural Shropshire, and to date all of our work has been made here. It then tours village halls and theatres locally and nationally. Over four and a half decades we've produced 173 new plays, reached over half a million audience members, won a prestigious South Bank Show award for our show about racism, a Fringe First for our play about climate change and were the first to livestream from a village hall. We have hosted a writer in residence since 2014, and they have gone on to be commissioned by the Royal Court, Birmingham Rep, Royal Welsh College, Nottingham Playhouse, HighTide and the Bush.

We are a champion for rural young people aged sixteen to twenty-five. Pentabus Young Company is our programme offering workshops, master classes, work experience and mentorships, as well as the opportunity to join our Young Writers Programme, which has been running for eight years. Previous participants of the Young Writers Programme have had their work presented at Ludlow Fringe, Latitude Festival and Hereford Courtyard. It is a springboard into further study and the arts industry, with many of our Young Writers going on to be published and professional writers.

You can find out more about us at:

pentabus.co.uk

Twitter: @pentabustheatre | Facebook: Pentabus Theatre
Instagram: Pentabustheatrecompany

Pentabus Theatre,
Bromfield, Ludlow, Shropshire SY8 2JU

Pentabus is also supported by the Adlard Family Charitable Foundation, the Ashley Family Foundation, the Clive & Sylvia Richards Charity, the D'Oyly Carte Charitable Trust, the Garrick Charitable Trust, Hall Garth Charitable Trust, the Haystack Trust, the Millichope Foundation, Pilotlight, Weston Charity Awards & the Wynn Foundation.

"The most beautifully located and friendly theatre in Britain."
– *The Independent*

Theatre by the Lake creates theatre which inspires, and is inspired by the communities and landscape of Cumbria. The theatre makes up to nine shows a year as well as hosting a variety of festivals and visiting companies across their two theatre spaces.

You can find out more about us at:

theatrebythelake.com

Twitter: @tbtlake | Facebook: @tbtlake

Theatre by the Lake
Lakeside, Keswick, Cumbria CA12 5DJ

Box Office: 017687 74411
www.theatrebythelake.com

Marketing & Sales

Head of Communications: Rachel Swift
Marketing Officer: Rachel Price

Production & Technical

Technical & Production Manager: Phil Geller
Stage Technician: Nicholas Wharton
Technician: Joshua Callaway
Technician: Adam Griggs
Assistant Technician: Connor Barton

CHARACTERS

OLIVIA DUDZAI – Thirty, though looks much younger. Black British woman of Zimbabwean heritage. She is an equine vet. Wife of Jimmy. Mother of Rudo.

MATTY TAYLOR – Fifty-three. White British man. Gamekeeper. Father of Ste and husband of Jan.

AUTHOR'S NOTES

Throughout the play, the usual rural night sounds can be heard. These rural sounds alternate at times between the sounds of rural Shropshire and the sounds of rural Zimbabwe at Lake Chivero and Lion and Cheetah Park in Harare. Whenever Lake Chivero is mentioned in stage directions, this also refers to Lion and Cheetah Park from Olivia's perspective. While these are two separate places in reality, they are combined to create a dreamlike soundscape in the play.

All music used should alternate between Zimbabwean mbira music and European music at appropriate moments.

As Olivia and Matty interact with them, particular stage spaces are designated as the location of the female curlew or curlew chicks.

/ within dialogue indicates interruption.

Jacaranda is dedicated to the loving memory of
Amai Inno, Rupert French and Clarissa Gangaidzo.

Jacaranda would not be the play it is without the generous support of all
at Pentabus Theatre and the wonderful Juliet Gilkes Romero.

ACT ONE

(Lights up. Night. 10:30 p.m. in the imaginary, small Shropshire rural village of Anchorton Forge. A small stream on the publicly accessible land at the back of Jacaranda Farm. Jacaranda farmhouse is visible. A grazing field of twelve to fifteen sheep and several lambs is between the farmhouse and the stream. A single light is on on the second floor of the farmhouse.)

(Other typical nighttime sounds of rural Shropshire can be heard.)

*(**OLIVIA**, thirty, a Black British woman, enters. She looks much younger than her age. She only has a thin top on and so hugs herself tightly with her right arm to keep warm. There is a large graze on one cheek. She holds her left arm at her side gingerly.)*

*(A vixen barks somewhere distant. This gets **OLIVIA**'s attention. She moves a little too quickly and jolts her left arm.)*

OLIVIA. Ah!

*(She stills for a few moments, letting the pain subside. **OLIVIA** takes her walking boots and socks off carefully, doing everything with her right hand. She sits with her feet in the gently flowing water. The water's cold, and she flinches at first and withdraws her feet, but*

*then plunges them back in and makes herself
endure it.)*

*(She shivers slightly, looking at the night sky.
She takes out her phone and records a video,
speaking to camera.)*

OLIVIA. Okay, so we're up to S. Let me see, S for, S for –
(Thinks.) S for Sky. *(Looks around.)* S for Stream. S for,
for, for um, for Sheep!

(She points the camera out to the audience.)

See baby, there they are: sheep. Well lambs and sheep.
See them all settled for the night? All fluffy and cozy.
Mommies there protecting their babies. Hear that faint
bubble of the stream. *(Turns the camera on the stream.)*
I like to think it's whispering stories all through the day
and all through the night for those who have the ears
to hear them. Stories of before now, stories I wanted to
hear with you. Stories I wanted to tell you. *(Beat.)* But
here; I can record them, hope you can hear them too.

(Beat.)

*(**OLIVIA**'s voice trembles with emotion.
Turning the camera skyward.)*

And that sky! Millions of years. Just there, watching.

*(Crickets join the other night sounds. They
are continuous; insistent and repetitive
sounds that would fill a Zimbabwean night.)*

*(**OLIVIA** turns the camera out to the audience
again and points to a different place.)*

See those hills over there, near where that ancient yew
tree is? I snuck up there once with Babamukuru George
when I was very small. The Long Mynd was ours on a
summer night like this; just him and me. The summer
my Baba died. Babamukuru George brought us out

here, Mum and I, so that we could just be he said; so we could breathe. Mum'd put me to bed, then when it got dark he came and got me and we snuck up there. Up to New Pool Hollow. We just looked at the stars; could see the Milky Way with all its billions of stars. Lay on our backs looking up and he told me stories. Stories I wanted to tell you. Of the most incredible sunsets that look like a sky on fire, of the Black House, of avenues of streets lined with gorgeous jacaranda flowers that make a carpet of purple for you to walk on. Jacarandas always make me think of him.

> *(Beat. A jackal calls in the distance.)*

> *(An elephant trumpets. She points her phone at a different spot in the audience and fiddles with her camera phone, changing from portrait to landscape. The sounds of Lake Chivero dominate during the following.)*

There, got it. So you can see more, see everything. See it there my little one, if you squint a bit? A great big elephant that is sweetheart. African elephant. Loved them as a kid. Babamukuru George took me to see some once. Mum had moved us to Zimbabwe then. Boxing Day him, me and Mum; *(Laughs at the memory.)* complaining that the heat felt like a real living thing wrapping itself around her, trying to kill her. Went to Lion and Cheetah Park, then on to Lake Chivero for a day out.

> *(**OLIVIA** gestures towards the elephant and winces as the movement impacts her injured left arm.)*

Look she's seen her calf! He's right there trotting after his mum! Can live to seventy you know, elephants. Got prickles all over his trunk that little calf. Looks smooth but it's not up close. Found that out Boxing Day. When you stop imagining what an elephant would feel like and take the time to really look, really feel. Should've had my window closed on the safari but I was so excited by all the animals. A baby elephant came up to the car. Put his trunk in the window and felt around a bit. He was still little, didn't know the danger. I did though. I tried to be brave and stroke his trunk. But I couldn't bring myself to. I wanted to...but...then Babamukuru George took my hand, guided me, you know. Felt so weird at first, feeling those prickles on my skin. *(Beat.)* I wanted to do that with you; take your tiny hand and help you to be brave like that. Help you be brave enough to really see things like that; not just imagine them but see them, feel them for yourself. *(Beat.)* Can you see them baby? They're faint, the picture's a bit unsteady sometimes but they're still there.

> *(A female curlew calls feebly.* **OLIVIA** *jumps, looks around but sees nothing. She briefly concentrates on the window with the light on at Jacaranda farmhouse and roughly wipes away a tear.)*

> *(The female elephant trumpets in the distance again.)*

(Speaking into the camera. Smiling broadly.) Hear that darling?

> *(***OLIVIA** *lays on her back, looking at the stars, with her feet in the stream. After a few moments she sits up and uses one of her socks to dry off her feet. It's difficult with one hand.)*

> *(A box of tablets falls out of* **OLIVIA**'s *jeans pocket. She looks at it, takes out one of the blister packs and examines it. She holds them to her and rocks. She's emotional. She gets up to put the box back in her pocket and steps on a pile of curlew feathers by mistake. She picks up a couple from the large pile of feathers. There's nothing there. She is about*

to leave when a single jacaranda flower blows in and lands in the pile of feathers. **OLIVIA** *notices it and picks up the flower, confused. She examines it carefully. She treats the jacaranda flower delicately and carefully tucks it into the box of tablets.* **OLIVIA** *puts the box of tablets back in her pocket.)*

(She uses a stick to scrape mud out of the tread of her boots. While she works, a few more jacaranda flowers land at her feet. She looks up in wonder, unsure where the flowers are coming from. She takes a picture of the jacaranda flowers among the curlew feathers.)

(She is collecting the flowers together as **MATTY,** *fifty-three, enters. He is dressed as a typical gamekeeper. He is carrying a side-by-side shotgun and a torch that is off.)*

*(***MATTY*** creeps up behind* **OLIVIA** *and aims his gun at her.)*

MATTY. Private land this is!

*(***OLIVIA*** jumps, sees* **MATTY** *and the gun. She cowers and covers her head.)*

S'pose they around; yer friends? Cuttin' the pens are they?

OLIVIA. *(Scrambles backwards.)* Woah! I...I...

MATTY. Clump me on the head, then let 'em all go; is that it?

*(***MATTY*** tries to appear utterly confident, but the hand holding the shotgun shakes slightly.)*

*(***OLIVIA*** notices and puts a hand up to shield herself.)*

      *(**MATTY** holds the gun steady with both hands.)*

OLIVIA. *(Whispers.)* Don't.

MATTY. If yer don't get yer shit together and leave now. With all yer friends! I'm calling the police.

OLIVIA. Please.

      *(**MATTY** stands over her.)*

      *(Openly crying and terrified now, **OLIVIA** hastily collects her boots and socks at the barrel of the shotgun.)*

MATTY. I know yer game. Not so big when yer friends ain't with yer are yer?

      *(**OLIVIA** remains silent.)*

Nearly wiped me out last year your lot! And I ain't havin' it again!

      *(Still barefoot, **OLIVIA** backs away from him slowly and carefully.)*

Bloody Antis! Think yer can just let my birds out, do yer? Keeps food on my table this, and yer pissin' about like it don't matter!

      *(**MATTY** takes a couple of steps towards **OLIVIA** with the shotgun. **OLIVIA** stops.)*

OLIVIA. Please! I'm not... /

      *(**MATTY** takes out his phone and starts dialling the police. He also turns on the torch and shines it at **OLIVIA**.)*

MATTY. Tell that to the poli– *(Stops dead as his torch illuminates **OLIVIA**'s face.)*

      *(**MATTY** takes a step backwards.)*

(**OLIVIA** *scrambles away from him immediately and cowers.*)

I...

OLIVIA. *(Desperate.)* Don't hurt me, don't hurt me, don't hurt me.

(*He realises he is still holding his gun and puts it down.*)

(*Beat.*)

(**MATTY** *goes to approach* **OLIVIA** *but thinks better of it.*)

(**OLIVIA,** *still terrified, risks a look at* **MATTY.**)

Let me go?

MATTY. *(Approaching* **OLIVIA.***)* I didn't mean...

(**OLIVIA** *desperately moves away.*)

No, yer don't have to do th... I /

OLIVIA. Don't know what's happ– /

MATTY. Yeah, I know and /

OLIVIA. Didn't know it's private land.

MATTY. It's not.

(**OLIVIA** *gives him a look.*)

Got it wrong. Got you wrong.

(**OLIVIA**'s *eyes are on the shotgun.* **MATTY** *notices and moves it farther away with his foot.*)

(*Beat.*)

It's only that...

(*Beat.*)

MATTY. I just…

OLIVIA. Should get going.

>   *(MATTY fully takes in the scared, barefoot woman in front of him.)*

MATTY. At least put yer boots on.

OLIVIA. It's fine.

MATTY. It's not.

>   *(Because of her injured arm, OLIVIA awkwardly puts down her boots and socks. MATTY notices OLIVIA's arm.)*

>   *(OLIVIA starts putting on her boots. One of the laces is undone and she struggles to do it up with one hand.)*

(Moving towards OLIVIA.) Need help? *(Stops dead as OLIVIA moves away.)*

(Beat. The two contemplate each other.)

Could give yer a hand. Only if yer want?

(Beat. MATTY waits.)

OLIVIA. Okay.

>   *(MATTY moves towards OLIVIA carefully, so as not to scare her. He ties the laces of her boot and then moves to sit a distance away from her.)*

MATTY. I'll sit here okay?

>   *(OLIVIA goes to leave.)*

Seen both of yer in the village last few months. You and him. Know you've moved in over at Jacaranda Farm… Old George's place.

OLIVIA. *(Turning back to* **MATTY.***)* Then why?

MATTY. Someone said there's lights up near the woods, could be Antis releasing my birds. Only had the chicks delivered yesterday. Keep my pheasants up this way. Didn't know it was you at first.

OLIVIA. Probably shouldn't be wandering around at night.

MATTY. Best not.

OLIVIA. I should – *(Goes to leave again.)*

MATTY. Sorry again.

> *(The call of an injured female curlew is heard. Both* **MATTY** *and* **OLIVIA** *register the sound.)*
>
> *(***MATTY** *picks up his shotgun and looks over to where the curlew call came from.)*
>
> *(***MATTY** *searches the area near the stream carefully and thoroughly. He suddenly finds an injured female curlew.)*

(Talking to the curlew.) Bloody hell. There she is. A curlew. What a beauty. Come on girl.

> *(***OLIVIA** *can't help but look back to see what* **MATTY** *has found.)*
>
> *(The female curlew calls again.)*
>
> *(***MATTY** *carefully tries to lift the curlew from the stream's edge.)*

(Softly to the female curlew.) Come on girl.

> *(The curlew struggles and cries out in distress.)*

OLIVIA. Don't hurt her!

MATTY. Never do that. Fox or somethin' must've got to her. She's stuck in the mud. Give me a hand?

OLIVIA. *(Shaking her head.)* Um, I've got to /

MATTY. Talk in the village is you're a vet.

OLIVIA. For horses.

MATTY. Come on. This here's a curlew. Endangered, not that many left now.

OLIVIA. *(Looks at her watch.)* Got to go. Going up Long Mynd.

MATTY. This time of night?

OLIVIA. Just up to New Pool Hollow.

> *(**OLIVIA** starts turning to go. More jacaranda flowers blow in on the wind. **OLIVIA** briefly notices them.)*

MATTY. She can't wait. *(Beat.)* Please.

> *(**OLIVIA** stands undecided for a moment. She unconsciously feels the outline of the box of tablets in her trouser pocket. Looks at the fresh Jacaranda petals on the ground.)*

> *(**OLIVIA** is reluctant to stay, but eventually moves towards **MATTY** and the curlew.)*

OLIVIA. You lift her.

MATTY. *(To the curlew.)* There girl. It's okay.

> *(**MATTY** takes off his coat.)*

> *(**OLIVIA** and **MATTY** carry the curlew from the stream to their position next to the wood. Actors are to improvise dialogue directed to the curlew during this action. The calm curlew is placed between **OLIVIA** and **MATTY**. Throughout the following, the curlew is mainly unresponsive, but very occasionally there are weak cries from it.)*

(The mixed-up sounds of rural Shropshire and rural Lake Chivero are heard throughout the following.)

(It is very important that there is only a suggestion that there is a curlew present. A particular space onstage is designated as the location of the curlew.)

Should take her back to yours. Warm her up.

OLIVIA. Can't.

MATTY. Yer s'posed to be a vet.

OLIVIA. Not set up yet. Your place?

MATTY. Can't.

> *(**MATTY** catches a bug and very gently tries to feed it to the curlew. She won't take it. **OLIVIA** watches him trying.)*

She's in a bad way.

OLIVIA. Can't work you out.

> *(**MATTY** keeps trying different tactics to get the curlew to eat, but it won't.)*

> *(**OLIVIA** takes **MATTY**'s coat and covers the curlew with it as **MATTY** speaks.)*

MATTY. Know yer type don't I. Seen yer and yer fella, always in the car drivin' up the lane there. Drivin' everywhere. Never wantin' to get yer feet mucky walkin' up to the village, or walkin' round here. Beautiful walks all over these hills yer know.

> *(**OLIVIA** ignores him.)*

OLIVIA. If it's endangered should call the RSPCA. *(Indicates the curlew.)* Get specialist care.

>   *(OLIVIA gets her phone out, unlocks it, and light from it illuminates her face, showing the graze on her cheek. MATTY sees it for the first time.)*

OLIVIA. Must be an out-of-hours place that'll come out?

MATTY. *(Laughs, but he's examining her face and injured arm.)* Can't just Google things out here. Take care of things ourselves. Gwen's got the rescue place, next village over. Be closed now, gotta be almost midnight.

OLIVIA. *(Suppresses her irritation at being laughed at.)* Must have an out-of-hours service?

MATTY. Yer not in the city now.

OLIVIA. – *(Irritated but suppresses it.)*

>   *(Beat. MATTY takes in OLIVIA's thin top and lack of even a sweater. OLIVIA shivers slightly.)*

MATTY. Done somethin' to yer arm then?

>   *(OLIVIA is a bit flustered.)*

OLIVIA. I'm fine.

MATTY. Cut on yer face; looks nasty.

>   *(OLIVIA touches her cheek, makes contact with the graze and winces.)*

OLIVIA. Tripped coming through the sheep pen.

MATTY. Yeah?

OLIVIA. Pitch-black out here.

MATTY. Moon's pretty bright now.

OLIVIA. Must of gone behind a cloud or something.

MATTY. Must of.

OLIVIA. Went down hard.

MATTY. Yeah?

OLIVIA. Yeah.

>   *(Beat.)*

MATTY. Come, I'll drive yer up to your place. Gonna need a doctor to look at that arm.

OLIVIA. Don't want to put you to any trouble.

MATTY. Happy to.

OLIVIA. *(Shaking her head.)* Really I /

MATTY. I insist.

OLIVIA. *(Too abruptly.)* No.

>   *(**MATTY** is surprised.)*

What I mean is, I know what I need.

MATTY. Yer in pain.

OLIVIA. I don't need anyone. I'm fine on my own.

MATTY. Yer a charmer. Okay, so if yer won't let me drive yer, at least let me call yer fella to come and get yer.

OLIVIA. Leave it okay?

>   *(Beat. **MATTY** thinks. **OLIVIA** briefly, unconsciously feels the outline of the box of tablets in her pocket.)*

Okay?

>   *(Beat.)*

MATTY. *(He's very awkward.)* If he's…uh…if he's yer know… hurtin' yer…maybe I could /

OLIVIA. *(Amazed.)* If he's what?

MATTY. Yer arm, yer face, just /

OLIVIA. No.

MATTY. Just thought maybe /

OLIVIA. No.

MATTY. Didn't mean /

OLIVIA. Know our type though, Jimmy and me, right?

MATTY. Only trying to /

OLIVIA. Know my type?

MATTY. No I /

OLIVIA. Without me even having to say a word.

>*(A moment.)*

He never would.

MATTY. Must think I'm an old fool.

OLIVIA. Know you meant well, I just /

MATTY. Can't seem to...gettin' it all wrong tonight.

OLIVIA. No, no, it's me, I'm overreacting.

MATTY. *(Extends his hand to shake* **OLIVIA***'s.)* Matthew, Matty to my mates.

>*(It's awkward, as* **OLIVIA** *doesn't shake his hand but goes to touch elbows instead.)*

OLIVIA. Olivia.

>*(***MATTY** *realises his mistake and touches elbows instead.)*

MATTY. Keep forgettin'. Shakin' hands is just what yer do isn't it?

OLIVIA. Not anymore.

MATTY. No.

OLIVIA. *(Indicating the curlew.)* She's stopped moving.

(MATTY goes over and checks on the curlew.)

MATTY. Must be still in shock.

> *(Beat. OLIVIA looks to the farmhouse, while MATTY carefully watches the curlew.)*

Her breathing's so slow.

OLIVIA. Give her time, takes hours for animals to recover from shock. And there's her wing.

> *(MATTY begins collecting branches and leaves to make a kind of nest for the curlew.)*

MATTY. Needs a warm nest and she'll be right as rain.

> *(OLIVIA doesn't move.)*

Give me a hand then.

> *(OLIVIA jumps up and begins to help gather leaves and small branches with her uninjured hand. She really puts effort into it. Together they build a nest for the curlew, with MATTY guiding OLIVIA on the layering of the branches on the bottom and then lining it with leaves. When they've finished, both look at it, pleased.)*

OLIVIA. Not too bad for a city girl.

MATTY. *(Reluctant admiration.)* Did pretty well.

> *(Encouraged, OLIVIA takes a packet of tissues from her trouser pocket and begins tucking them around the curlew.)*

Oi, what yer doin' messin' with all that now?

OLIVIA. Chick fell from a tree in the garden once when I was a kid. Dominic, our gardener, showed me. Lined a shoebox with tissues. It helps.

MATTY. Hold on a minute; who's the one who knows what he's doing here and now?

OLIVIA. Just thought /

> *(As he speaks, MATTY picks out the few tissues and screws them up into a ball that he puts in his trouser pocket.)*

MATTY. Don't need this lot. Yer just listen to me and she'll be fine. Been workin' pheasants thirty odd years. I know my birds.

OLIVIA. Okay then Dr Do Little, what next?

> *(MATTY gives her a look.)*

Well.

> *(The sound of a vixen a little closer than before. OLIVIA looks in the direction it came from.)*

(Laughing.) Not gonna hurt yer.

OLIVIA. Think I'm scared of a fox?

> *(Rustling comes from the woods. Pheasant chicks call to alert others. MATTY's head snaps in the direction of the sound.)*

> *(OLIVIA becomes aware that MATTY's on alert and something is wrong.)*

What is it?

> *(MATTY puts his fingers to his lips. His attention is on the wood nearby where the noises came from.)*

(Whispers.) What?

MATTY. *(Whispers.)* Could be Antis in the pheasant pen.

> (**MATTY** *goes to retrieve his gun.* **OLIVIA** *sees what he's going to do and grabs it before he can get to it.*)

> (*More rustling is heard from the wood.*)

What the hell are yer doing?

> (**OLIVIA** *holds the gun on him. She's scared of everything, but she holds the gun level at him with her good arm.*)

Olivia, they'll let the chicks out. That'll be the end for me!

OLIVIA. *(Shouting into the woods with all her might.)* Run! He's got a gun!

> (**MATTY** *comes towards* **OLIVIA** *slowly.*)

MATTY. *(As calmly as he can.)* Look, this is silly. Just put the gun /

> (**OLIVIA** *cocks the shotgun. Awkwardly and painfully, with help from her injured arm.*)

> (**MATTY** *stops in his tracks, and the two face off.*)

> (*A few alerted pheasant chicks in the wood can be heard.*)

> (*A lot of rustling comes from the wood. The disturbed, urgent voices of* **THREE ANTIS** *are heard coming from the wood. A few pheasant chicks continue to call.*)

ANTI 1. *(Voice-over.)* Come on!

ANTI 2. *(Voice-over.)* Just leave it!

ANTI 3. *(Voice-over.)* Go! Go!

(Noise of the three running from the wood during the following.)

MATTY. Come on now. They're gettin' away.

*(**OLIVIA** stands firm with the shotgun aimed at **MATTY**.)*

(Maybe the sounds of car doors being slammed a short distance away, or some other sign the three have left. The pheasant chicks quiet down again quite quickly.)

*(**OLIVIA** visibly relaxes and lets the gun barrel drop a little.)*

*(**MATTY** advances.)*

*(Unsure what to do now, **OLIVIA** retreats a step. She tries to hold the gun steady at **MATTY** again, but by now she's getting emotional and shaking too much.)*

*(**MATTY** advances again.)*

*(**OLIVIA**, still shaking, dissolves to her knees.)*

*(Confident now, **MATTY** comes and grabs the gun.)*

*(**OLIVIA** puts a hand up in anticipation of physical retaliation.)*

Stupid bitch!

*(**OLIVIA** sits and cries.)*

*(**MATTY** puts the shotgun well out of **OLIVIA**'s reach.)*

*(**MATTY** exits to check on his pheasant chicks. The sound of a few pheasant chick calls are audible.)*

(OLIVIA visibly relaxes.)

(MATTY enters from the wood.)

(Looks at OLIVIA with hatred.) Who the fuck asked you to interfere?!

> *(OLIVIA braves a look at MATTY, sees the look in his eyes, and buries her head in her hands a moment.)*

OLIVIA. Couldn't let you shoot them, could I?

MATTY. Wouldn't have.

OLIVIA. Couldn't know that.

MATTY. Yer don't know. That's the thing. I know! I know and yer don't! Gun was to protect, not attack. Protect my birds.

> *(Beat.)*

OLIVIA. When you pointed it at me, didn't know if you would or not.

MATTY. Don't be stupid.

OLIVIA. Whatever they're doing out here, can't just go waving guns at them.

MATTY. That what livin' in London, or wherever taught yer, is it? Comin' out here, buyin' up land, and yer want to tell me how to live?

OLIVIA. No I /

MATTY. Yer wanna know why I take a gun out with me now?

> *(MATTY pulls up his jumper to expose a large scar across his stomach. OLIVIA gasps.)*

Stuck me with wire cutters last year. Let the pheasants out and stuck me when I tried to stop 'em.

(A moment.)

OLIVIA. Someone did that to me, I'd be scared too. But is a gun the /

MATTY. They don't scare me.

OLIVIA. Sorry, didn't mean /

MATTY. They're just idiots runnin' around the countryside tryin' to stop the hunts and the shoot days. No thought about what that does to people like me, relyin' on things like that for their livin'. Scared? No way.

OLIVIA. Maybe if you try to see their side / then –

MATTY. What?

OLIVIA. Yeah they're different to you but /

MATTY. Yeah, and I've got the scars to prove it.

OLIVIA. Might not be so hostile / if you both –

MATTY. What yer know about it?

OLIVIA. Nothing but /

MATTY. That's what I thought.

> *(**OLIVIA** ignores **MATTY** and starts caring for the curlew. She takes the leaves she has collected and gently tries to put them around the bird to keep her warm.)*
>
> *(The curlew calls weakly to warn her off.)*
>
> *(**MATTY** clocks this as he listens carefully for any sounds coming from the wood.)*
>
> *(The curlew gives a weak cry and drags itself back to the edge of the stream.)*
>
> *(Both **MATTY** and **OLIVIA** watch the curlew return to the same place in the undergrowth at the edge of the stream.)*

Even the bloody curlew thinks she knows better than I do!

>   *(Beat.)*

OLIVIA. Did any pheasants /

MATTY. Didn't get into the pen. No thanks to you.

OLIVIA. –

>   *(**MATTY** tries to check on the female curlew. It calls even more weakly to warn him off.)*

Got to put pressure on that wound. Probably want to cauterise that slight bleed. But pressure's all we've got out here.

MATTY. Go on then.

OLIVIA. Well she's...

MATTY. Yer seem to know what's best.

>   *(**OLIVIA** approaches the female curlew a couple of times, but it resists her. She has to retreat both times. **MATTY** laughs at her.)*

OLIVIA. Help me.

>   *(**OLIVIA** tries one more time. She gets the closest to holding the wing with a tissue that she has so far, but the curlew again resists – even weaker still. **OLIVIA** goes to retreat again.)*

>   *(**MATTY** gives **OLIVIA** a look.)*

>   *(**MATTY** takes off the jacket and uses one of the balled-up tissues to apply some pressure to the curlew's wing to stem the still slightly bleeding wound. The exhausted bird has no fight left and so lets him.)*

MATTY. Burdock's good for this. Stop it gettin' infected. Thought I saw some by the water.

OLIVIA. Wound just needs firm pressure for five minutes or so.

MATTY.   Burdock's ancient wisdom. Passed down generations. Not everythin' yer need to know's from books.

OLIVIA. I'm not saying that, I /

MATTY. No use doin' this if it gets infected. Foxes are riddled with disease.

OLIVIA. S'what I'd do with a horse's wound.

MATTY. Funny-lookin' horse this.

OLIVIA. Principle's the same.

>   (**MATTY** *stops putting pressure on the curlew's wing.*)

MATTY. Yer wanna try?

OLIVIA. *(Rolls her eyes.)* Fine. Burdock you said?

>   (**OLIVIA** *goes to the stream and turns on her phone's torch to light the way.*)

MATTY. Ha!

>   (**OLIVIA** *looks at plants near the stream briefly.*)

Starvin'.

OLIVIA. *(Returning sheepishly.)* Which one's burdock?

MATTY. *(Laughs.)* Flat green leaves, pink spiky flowers.

OLIVIA. Stop laughing at me.

>   (**MATTY** *checks through all of his pockets. He finds a comb and assorted sweets. He combs his hair a few times and then looks through his finds.*)

MATTY.   Okay, so we've got a Mini Twix, two Mars Celebrations and one last polo. What can I do yer for?

OLIVIA.   I'm okay.

MATTY.   *(Unwrapping a Celebration.)* Sure yer don't want one?

> *(**OLIVIA** shakes her head.)*

More for me then. *(Popping the chocolate in his mouth and chewing.)* Ah proper nice. Haven't eaten since tea.

OLIVIA.   *(To remember it.)* Pink spiky flowers, pink spiky flowers.

MATTY.   *(Calling after her.)* That's the one.

> *(**OLIVIA** returns to the stream and searches with the light from her phone torch. **MATTY** eats the mini Twix and then the polo. He pockets the comb and the Mars Celebration.)*
>
> *(**OLIVIA** searches briefly and trips on a rock and hurts her left leg. She hops on her uninjured leg as she returns to the curlew and **MATTY**. **MATTY** laughs at how ridiculous **OLIVIA** looks hopping.)*
>
> *(**OLIVIA** gives him a disapproving look.)*

(Still laughing.) Yer don't know how funny yer are. Should take a picture.

> *(**MATTY** tries to control his laughter but is unable to.)*
>
> *(**OLIVIA** has spotted something.)*

OLIVIA.   Oh no.

> *(**OLIVIA** picks up the curlew's nest she has found and arrives back to where **MATTY** is now doubled over with laughter at her. Being*

> *careful to put it out of the female curlew's*
> *sight,* **OLIVIA** *silences* **MATTY** *by carefully and*
> *gently placing the curlew nest near him. The*
> *nest contains three seemingly dead curlew*
> *chicks.* **MATTY** *stops laughing and is horrified.*
> *The audience does not see the chicks.)*

MATTY. What's wrong with yer, showing me that?

> *(The sound of the female mother elephant*
> *trumpeting in distress. The sound of jackals*
> *barking with the thrill and excitement of*
> *chasing prey.)*

> *(***OLIVIA*** looks out into the audience where the*
> *mother elephant and her cub are positioned.)*

OLIVIA. Can you hear that?

MATTY. *(Listens.)* Hear what?

OLIVIA. Oh it doesn't matter.

> *(There is one last, short distressed call from*
> *the mother elephant that is drowned out by*
> *the vicious sound of jackals.)*

> *(***MATTY*** moves away from the nest.)*

> *(***OLIVIA*** remains where she is and is focussed*
> *on the nest now and cannot look away.)*

MATTY. Don't look. It's horrible.

OLIVIA. *(Her eyes fixed on the nest.)* Nature's so cruel. If
this injured mother curlew lays her three eggs, can
keep them warm; incubate them for weeks 'til they
hatch, the least we can do is look at her dead babies.

> *(Beat.)*

> *(***MATTY*** takes some sticks and leaves from*
> *those piled up in the nest they made for the*

curlew and, as gently as possible, uses them to cover up the nest with the three dead curlew chicks.)

MATTY. *(Looking down at the curlew.)* Imagine that; curlew pair mated for life and a fox comes along and blows it all up; chicks and all. Just fuckin' heartbreakin'.

> *(**OLIVIA** looks up to Jacaranda farmhouse and the one room with a light on. A silhouette of Jimmy can be seen in that room now.)*

OLIVIA. Yeah. Fucking heartbreaking.

> *(**MATTY** follows her gaze.)*

MATTY. Fight with yer fella bring yer out here?

OLIVIA. Told you I fell.

MATTY. Know what yer said.

OLIVIA. I can't just go for a walk if I want to?

MATTY. Walkin' around barefoot with nothing warm on, this time of night?

OLIVIA. Forgot, you know all about people like me.

> *(The box of tablets falls out of her trouser pocket. **MATTY** picks up the box of tablets and reads it. **OLIVIA** grabs the box as quickly as she can and shoves it back in her pocket.)*

MATTY. *(Suspicious now.)* Why're yer out here?

OLIVIA. Doesn't matter.

MATTY. With a box of those?

> *(Her gaze is back on the dead chicks in the curlew nest.)*

OLIVIA. –

MATTY. Olivia?

OLIVIA. Matthew?

MATTY. What're the pills for?

OLIVIA. –

> *(Suddenly, some rustling leaves are heard just behind them in the wood.* OLIVIA's *attention does not waver from the nest. A single chick moves slightly in the nest.)*

One of the chicks, he moved! He's moving!

> *(Straight after* OLIVIA's *announcement, the sound of twigs breaking and something approaching can be heard behind them.* MATTY *grabs for his gun, picks it up, swings around.)*

> *(*OLIVIA *jumps up and tries to take the gun from* MATTY. *She is not strong enough to overpower him and take the gun, but she holds onto it anyway as long as she can.)*

Can't!

MATTY. Get off!

OLIVIA. Can't just go after people. I'm not scared of you!

> *(As the lights go down a shot goes off.* OLIVIA *screams.)*

ACT TWO

(Lights up. Same setting. **OLIVIA** *is present. She is breathing heavily from her struggle for the shotgun. She paces, anxious to know if the bullet injured any Antis.)*

*(**MATTY** enters with the gun, having shot a vixen in the wood.)*

*(**MATTY** rolls his eyes.)*

OLIVIA. Who was it?

MATTY. Vixen, that's all it was.

OLIVIA. *(Relaxes a little.)* You didn't know that.

MATTY. Probably one who attacked her. *(Indicates the female curlew.)*

(Beat.)

OLIVIA. Vixen, she in pain?

MATTY. No.

OLIVIA. You sure?

MATTY. One shot and that was it, don't worry.

OLIVIA. She have cubs you think?

MATTY. Might do. Foxes are vermin though. End of.

OLIVIA. Matters to me if she has cubs.

*(**OLIVIA** tries to feed a worm to the curlew chick. He won't take it, but she keeps trying.)*

(Beat.)

(OLIVIA disassembles the shotgun, puts each of the three pieces in different places. MATTY watches her.)

MATTY. Yer not right. Whatever's gone on with you – *(Indicates Jacaranda farmhouse.)* Yer don't grab at a shotgun that way. One of us could have been killed.

OLIVIA. But lashing out's right? Aiming at anyone? Shooting at anyone?

MATTY. And goin' up the Mynd with them pills ain't an answer.

OLIVIA. Don't know what you... To help me sleep that's all.

(Beat.)

(MATTY begins digging a hole with a stick.)

What're you / doing?

MATTY. *(Indicating the chicks.)* Gotta bury 'em.

OLIVIA. *(Protective, to the chick.)* Not you, you're weak but...you'll get stronger.

(OLIVIA very, very gently lifts the living chick and puts him on the nest they built earlier for the adult female curlew.)

(OLIVIA sits between MATTY and the living chick.)

MATTY. If we don't bury 'em you know predators'll get 'em.

(OLIVIA considers this a moment and then starts to dig a hole of her own.)

(MATTY and OLIVIA are digging a hole each, using a stick. MATTY's hole has progressed further than OLIVIA's.)

(OLIVIA stops digging a moment.)

OLIVIA. *(Indicating the two dead chicks.)* Look at them. They're so tiny. Fragile.

> *(MATTY looks up from the hole he has almost finished.)*

MATTY. I can do this, if yer…

OLIVIA. *(Slightly teary.)* No, I want to.

MATTY. I know people down in London yer think /

OLIVIA. You don't know what /

MATTY. Seen it for years. Day trippers doin' nature walks every summer. All over the place, lovin' the beauty of it out here. Lovin' themselves for bein' able to see the beauty in it, for gettin' back to nature. Sometimes though they forget nature can also be cruel, can be hard work and /

OLIVIA. *(Focussed on the dead chicks.)* I don't forget.

> *(Beat.)*

Can't forget.

> *(OLIVIA commences digging with renewed energy, getting more and more upset, until she throws down the stick.)*

I want to forget but… *(She is far away.)* He didn't even live for a moment. Just up here, you know? *(She touches her head.)* I imagine what he'd be like now. In two years, in five years, in ten years. What would his favourite colour be? His favourite food? Can't turn off my brain. *(A moment.)* Tomorrow's his due date, and we – *(Looks at her watch.)* No, it's past midnight. Today's the day he should have – *(Can't continue.)* Twenty-first of June 2021. But he was so tiny…so fragile…only twenty-eight weeks and suddenly he stopped moving inside me.

So three months ago it was 4:46 in the morning *(She needs a moment.)* and we were holding him. Too early. Too tiny.

(Beat.)

(She begins slowly but gets increasingly faster.) When I'm alone, the days Jimmy commutes; I wonder, you know? How his little face would have changed by now. His little hands and feet. *(A moment.)* They let us sit with him at the hospital. Looked like he was sleeping. Thought I'd want pictures, you know? For after. But I can't bring myself to – *(Can't continue.)* Jimmy can't stop looking. *(She looks at the single window with a light on at Jacaranda Farm.)* Every night he's up in what should be his nursery with the pictures of our boy. With the casts the hospital made for us of his hands and feet. Keep telling him I need to move on, put away the nursery things. The crib. The clothes. The tiny blue blanket with an elephant in one corner. *(She thinks for a few moments.)* But Jimmy won't. I just can't cope with all that. Is it normal d'you think? Thinking like this?

MATTY. I don't really... I'm not the one to... *(Trails off.)*

(Beat.)

OLIVIA. Scattered his ashes on the farm. Babamukuru George organised it all just before he – *(Can't say it.)*

MATTY. Good bloke was Old George. My family's doctor for years. Lots of people's round here.

OLIVIA. It was so sudden. Massive heart attack.

MATTY. Gutted when I heard.

OLIVIA. One day he was here, and then *(She clicks her fingers.)* just like that.

MATTY. Must be...

(Sounds of Lake Chivero dominate during the following.)

OLIVIA. Wanted our boy close; with family. Jimmy and I move here to raise our boy on the farm. I can start up my own practice. All of us be company for Babamukuru George. Raise our boy like I was raised in Zimbabwe, you know? Five years as a kid over there; seven years old and one day London's a memory and everything's new and /

MATTY. Bloody hell Zimbabwe; must've been tough?

OLIVIA. *(Speaks with wonder at the memories.)* Wasn't to me. There was just so much space. Had loads of fruit trees in the garden, kept chickens and ducks and turkeys. Went on safaris; saw animals I'd only ever seen on TV. And there was proper fresh air, you know? And oh man, horses / every Friday –

MATTY. Mugabe! That's right isn't it? In Zimbabwe?

OLIVIA. Mnangagwa now.

MATTY. Sure I saw something about Mugabe though?

OLIVIA. Chess club, girl guides and riding club were my three obsessions. Only horses and chess stuck when we came back to England /

MATTY. Seen it on the news; ran the country into the ground didn't he?

OLIVIA. News only ever tells you parts.

(A moment.)

MATTY. Sorry I... I'm sorry for yer loss. Yer boy and Old Ge– *(Thinks better of it.)* What did yer call him?

OLIVIA. Babamukuru George.

MATTY. Never heard him called that.

OLIVIA. A Shona name. Term of respect.

MATTY. Does it have a meaning then?

OLIVIA. Baba means father /

MATTY. Thought he was yer uncle?

OLIVIA. He was, but in Shona we'd say Babamukuru. Means big father; coz he was my dad's older brother. He's my vadzimu now...kind of like an ancestral spirit. Protects and guides. It's complicated.

MATTY. *(Thinks a moment.)* Somethin' nice about that. Big father. Still here.

　　　　*(**MATTY** gives **OLIVIA** a look.)*

OLIVIA. Don't do that.

MATTY. *(Looks away.)* Do what?

OLIVIA. I know that look. Try not to talk about my boy now...makes people uncomfortable. But sometimes... sometimes – *(A moment – she's emotional.)* Something happens, makes me think of him. Maybe I shouldn't but *(She exhales deeply at having to explain this.)* I say I lost him and it's looks like yours and no one knows what to say.

　　　　(A moment.)

Should keep it to myself.

MATTY. No.

OLIVIA. Doesn't change anything talking about it.

MATTY. Might help.

OLIVIA. Help who tho– /

MATTY. You.

　　　　*(**OLIVIA** gives **MATTY** a look.)*

I mean... If yer want...to talk I mean.

OLIVIA. I... Er...um...

MATTY. Only if you /

OLIVIA. *(Unsure she's doing the right thing.)* Yeah?

MATTY. Yeah.

> *(Beat. A few jacaranda leaves flutter down and land in and around the nest of dead curlew chicks.* **OLIVIA** *sees this. The elephant trumpets, and* **OLIVIA** *registers it.)*

OLIVIA. *(She takes a deep breath and exhales.)* If he was here I'd tell my boy a story about...there was this ice cream parlour in Harare Babamukuru George used to take me to the last Friday of every month without fail. This place, it was called Happy Days. There'd be ice cream cones covered with pink sprinkles or green sprinkles or honeycomb. Even though he was so busy at the hospital he always made the time once a month for a Pink Panther or Green Mamba or Crunchie ice cream with me. That's how he was. I thought I'd get the chance of that, of happy days like that with my boy.

> *(* **OLIVIA** *looks over to check on the living chick and unconsciously holds the box of sleeping pills in her pocket.* **MATTY** *sees.)*

MATTY. Could hold on to those, if yer want. Got lots a deep pockets.

OLIVIA. You're alright.

> *(* **MATTY** *opens a pocket on his combat trousers to demonstrate as he talks.)*

MATTY. See plenty a space. Keep 'em safe for yer.

OLIVIA. It's fine.

MATTY. Just thinkin' maybe /

OLIVIA. *(Indicating the holes.)* Let's get this done.

MATTY. If it's... I mean, if yer... I don't mind doin' it.

OLIVIA. No.

>*(Both **OLIVIA** and **MATTY** are ready to put a chick in each of the holes. **OLIVIA** tries hard to handle them but finds that when it comes to it she cannot pick up the dead chicks at all.)*

>*(Seeing her distress, **MATTY** steps in and gently puts the two chicks into the holes; one in each.)*

Maybe they should be together?

>*(**MATTY** moves one chick so that both are in the same grave. **MATTY** begins to cover both chicks over with dirt while **OLIVIA** turns away, unable to face it. **MATTY** stops filling in the graves.)*

I'm being silly.

MATTY. Yer not.

OLIVIA. I am. I'm not brave.

MATTY. Coulda fooled me.

OLIVIA. Couldn't even bury the chicks.

MATTY. So what?

OLIVIA. Don't have it in me to fight for my family. Hiding out here from Jimmy.

MATTY. Stood up to me though didn't yer?

OLIVIA. That's different.

MATTY. Took guts.

OLIVIA. Look, I should get going or I'll miss it.

MATTY. Miss what?

>*(Beat.)*

OLIVIA. 4:46.

> *(Beat.)*

MATTY. Stay here.

OLIVIA. Can't.

MATTY. Let it go by. *(Indicating the female curlew and chick.)* These two need yer.

OLIVIA. You got it handled.

MATTY. Need yer help to pick her up if I have to. Might get stuck in the mud again.

OLIVIA. Probably won't.

MATTY. *(Indicating the curlew chick.)* Saw yer lookin', checkin' on him.

OLIVIA. Matty I'm not brave like you. Out here protecting your birds from Antis. Protecting curlews from foxes.

MATTY. *(Indicating the curlew chick.)* Should get some food into this little guy.

> *(To Olivia.)* Help me?

>> *(There is a real pull on* **OLIVIA** *here to feed the baby chick. A moment where she decides.* **OLIVIA** *uses her phone's torch to search the ground for insects for the chick.)*

>> *(***MATTY** *uses his torch to join her in searching for insects.)*

> Gotcha!

MATTY. Yeah.

>> *(***OLIVIA** *catches a beetle and tries to feed it to the curlew chick. The chick won't take it, so* **OLIVIA** *places it within reach of the chick and watches.)*

MATTY. *(Holding a worm triumphantly.)* You tuck into that. Make you big and strong.

> *(**MATTY** places the worm in easy reach of the curlew chick.)*

OLIVIA. *(Pleading.)* You need to eat little one; so you can be strong enough to walk. And to fly. You want your beak to grow don't you? Eat baby; you want it to be long and strong so you can poke about for food.

MATTY. I think he's – *(Can't say that to her.)*

> *(The chick has died. **OLIVIA** watches it for a moment. She wipes away a tear.)*

OLIVIA. No, no, he's looking better I think. Brighter.

MATTY. –

> *(Quite a few jacaranda flowers blow in and cascade about the place.)*

OLIVIA. *(Desperate now.)* Matty, if we can just get enough of these insects into him I think Rudo's going to grow big and strong.

> *(**OLIVIA** claps her hand over her mouth.)*

> *(**MATTY** covers the dead curlew chick with more leaves and twigs from the nest they made.)*

OLIVIA. Haven't said his name since he – *(Can't bring herself to say it.)* Jimmy thinks I'm doing it on purpose but…it's the strangest thing…just couldn't say it.

> *(**MATTY** attempts to hug her, but she won't let him.)*

(Taking the leaves and twigs off the dead curlew chick.) Need to, need to just…

(**OLIVIA** *tries to pick up the curlew chick and is frustrated that she can't make herself.*)

MATTY. *(Moving to pick up the curlew chick.)* Let me /

OLIVIA. No I...

(**MATTY** *stops and watches.*)

(**OLIVIA** *gathers everything in her and slowly, slowly is able to delicately hold the dead chick in both hands. It's physically painful because of her injured arm and emotionally painful because of Rudo, but she manages to do it.* **OLIVIA** *carefully carries the chick to the grave of the other chicks and gently places him with them.* **MATTY** *gives her a thumbs up.*)

D'you think she knows?

MATTY. Maybe. Hope not.

(*During the following, the grave of the three chicks is fully filled in by* **MATTY** *and* **OLIVIA**. *They also fill in the other hole. Between them they fashion a cross out of two sticks and put it on top of the grave with the three chicks in it.* **OLIVIA** *then puts the first jacaranda flower she found on top of the grave to represent funeral flowers.*)

(**MATTY** *looks at what they have done together. He adjusts the cross slightly.* **OLIVIA** *finds a bug and puts it near the female curlew – staying out of her personal space as much as she can.*)

(*The curlew eats it.* **MATTY** *is overjoyed.*)

That's it girl.

(**OLIVIA** *gets up to leave.*)

Just stay 'til she's stronger.

OLIVIA. She's already on the mend.

MATTY. I'm not as brave as yer think. Yer right; Antis scare
me to death.

OLIVIA. I know what you're trying to do.

MATTY. It's true.

OLIVIA. It's okay.

MATTY. How can it be? What would yer Ba-ba...what was
it?

OLIVIA. Babamukuru.

MATTY. What'd he say about yer goin' up the Mynd?

> *(She smiles reassuringly at* MATTY, *checks her
> watch and starts to leave.)*

Want to know why I can't go home? Hit my boy tonight.
Grown man against a fourteen-year-old. How brave's
that?

> *(*OLIVIA, *horrified, stops and turns to face*
> MATTY.)*

Stay.

OLIVIA. Stop, okay?

MATTY. Wasn't lyin'.

OLIVIA. You're just trying to /

MATTY. I'm not.

> *(Beat.)*

OLIVIA. You're lying.

MATTY. –

OLIVIA. *(Indicating the female curlew.)* I've seen you;
you're so gentle with her.

MATTY. Wasn't gentle with you; not at first.

OLIVIA. People lash out when they're scared.

MATTY. Don't get scared.

OLIVIA. Said you did.

MATTY. Said that for you. Wanted to... *(Can't explain.)*

OLIVIA. Lied.

MATTY. No. Didn't mean... Why're yer excusin' it?

OLIVIA. Just trying to understand.

MATTY. Why're yer excusin' me?

OLIVIA. I'm not.

>	*(A moment.)*

MATTY. Have a go.

OLIVIA. What?

MATTY. Call me names.

OLIVIA. No.

MATTY. Why not? I deserve it.

>	*(**OLIVIA** thinks for a moment.)*

OLIVIA. Thug. Animal killer. Abuser.

>	*(A moment. **MATTY** closes his eyes.)*

MATTY. Man hits his kid there's only one thing to say.

OLIVIA. Said that for you. Don't really think /

MATTY. Yer should.

OLIVIA. Why? Did he say that; your son?

MATTY. Never said a word, Jan neither. Just gave me this look, both of 'em. Like they didn't know who I was. Had to get out of there.

>	*(Beat.)*

MATTY. Never laid a hand on Ste before. Swear I haven't.
What you've lost and I'm – *(Can't bring himself to say it.)*

OLIVIA. People don't just suddenly…something must've
happened / and –

MATTY. Why d'yer have to try to make it better? Can't. I'm
not what you think. *(He's far away, remembering.)* Yer
don't know my boy and me. Likes to bake, Ste. Should
say loves it. Always buyin' food I've never heard of.
Saves up his money for ingredients. Don't understand
it yer know. Three generations of gamekeepers in my
family and he's bakin'.

   (Beat.)

Heard there were lights up in the woods. Wanted him
to come check on the pheasant chicks with me. The way
he looked at me when I asked. Told him, don't know
why I bother askin' anymore. Been over a year since he
helped out with the pheasants. Never does anythin' at
all out with me now. I mean, well, bakin' and that's for
girls, isn't it? Think I could tell Trev or the lads down
the pub that my boy's made me a nice apple pie? Can't
trap a rabbit, got no clue how to set up the drinkers or
care for the poults, but he makes a cracking Victoria
sponge. When I was his age best times I had was
gettin' stuck in with Old Dez learnin' how to rear them
pheasants, sort out the foxes and weasels tryin' to get at
the birds. Back-breakin' work but good enough for Old
Dez, good enough for Ste's grandad too, good enough
for me. But him, he's too good for that. Got it in his
head he's gonna be some kind of pastry chef. Told him;
gonna start callin' him Stephanie the amount of bakin'
he does. Afraid to get his hands dirty like a real man,
that's his problem.

   (Beat.)

First time ever he's in my face, askin'; 'If yer such a real
man, so proud of what yer do, why d'yer lie about it?'

(*Beat.*)

I hit 'im. It was silly. Saw the fear on his face. Fear of me. Can't take it back. (*A moment.*) See, last summer I'm up in the village there. Met a young lad comin' out the co-op. Says he's lookin' for work, asks what I do. I say farmer, don't know why... I'm proud, course I am, it's just with some people, say gamekeeper, they react. Think they know me. Don't wait to find out; just tell me I'm a monster. Shoutin', 'Yer despicable,' 'Yer just love to slaughter animals,' 'Yer sick,' 'Murderous swine.' Animal killer you said.

OLIVIA. Didn't mean it. You know I didn't.

MATTY. Plenty of people mean it. Can get nasty.

OLIVIA. That why you don't say?

MATTY. Just to keep the peace like.

OLIVIA. We're not so different; Jimmy said the same. Said I lose myself coz I'd rather keep the peace. Said our boy'd be ashamed of me. Said that's why he's leaving.

MATTY. Ste just came out with it. Said he saw the lad, heard me deny gamekeepin' and didn't wanna know after that. Told him it was just to keep the peace. Didn't really matter. Said he used to think I was brave. Said he was ashamed. (*Balls up his fists.*) And I just – (*Can't continue.*)

(*A moment.*)

OLIVIA. Doesn't fear make us all act in funny ways? Can't always know what you'll /

(**MATTY** *starts collecting the sections of the shotgun and reassembling it as he speaks.*)

MATTY. Keep tellin' yer I'm not scared of them Antis. Said that to keep yer off the Mynd. What've I gotta be scared of?

OLIVIA. With your boy, maybe /

MATTY. Don't know what yer talkin' about. Gamekeepin's an ancient profession. Need guts to do it. Can't be scared of yer own shadow and do that. Used to be employed by kings; gamekeepers. Employed by the lord that owns the estate now I am. Do yer know that gamekeepers like me go back to medieval times? On this land; generations of my family.

(*Beat.*)

OLIVIA. Why d'you mock him?

MATTY. What?

OLIVIA. Ste?

MATTY. I don't.

OLIVIA. You do and it's horrible. Stephanie?

MATTY. (*Dismissive.*) Ah, he doesn't mind.

OLIVIA. How d'you know?

MATTY. He'd have said.

OLIVIA. Maybe he's like his dad; not saying, trying to keep the peace.

(*Silence.* **MATTY** *thinks.* **OLIVIA** *tends to the female curlew. It is perking up even more.*)

MATTY. So what do I do?

OLIVIA. Talk, maybe try to /

MATTY. I try hard with him.

OLIVIA. Try harder. Understand his side. Ask him what he likes to bake, why he likes it. Really really listen to the answer. Does he have to be you? Do what you do? Like what you like?

(*Beat.*)

MATTY. *(Awkward.)* So, um, yer not still thinkin' a goin' up the Mynd?

OLIVIA. –

MATTY. Really askin'.

OLIVIA. –

MATTY. Tryin' to understand.

> *(**OLIVIA** unconsciously holds the box of tablets in her pocket. **MATTY** notices.)*

Gotta talk to someone; talk to Jimmy. In and out of hospital Ste was when he was little. Really poorly. I know it's not the same. But when we, Jan and I, so many times we were scared to death Ste might – *(Still can't bring himself to say it.)* Back then we never stopped talkin'. Felt like we couldn't yer know? Like somethin' would break if we did.

> *(Beat.)*

OLIVIA. You were right before; I keep excusing people. *(Beat.)* Jimmy hates that about me; that I don't speak up. Says our boy would be ashamed of me. He's right. I'm ashamed of me. Can't live here he says. Can't ever have another baby with someone like me. Someone who wouldn't speak up for our child.

> *(Beat.)*

MATTY. He's wrong; Jimmy.

OLIVIA. What?

MATTY. You spoke up for my boy.

OLIVIA. You don't understand this.

MATTY. Understand Stephanie's pretty shitty.

> *(A moment.)*

MATTY. So I'm askin'.

OLIVIA. What?

MATTY. *(Unsure.)* Because it feels...feels like...I need to hear yer side. *(Beat.)* Yer speak up for my boy, speak up for Antis. But Jimmy's sayin' you don't speak up, you're excusin' things? I don't... The Mynd's a bastard to climb in the dark. Look, now if yer go up to New Pool Hollow I'll have to follow yer so...

> *(Beat.)*

OLIVIA. It feels...sometimes it's...so exposing...just walking in the village. No one has to ask me what I do before they're staring, thinking they know everything that I am. I drive into the village now. Not because of the mud. Don't mind mud, neither does Jimmy. I won't walk in because eyes on me like that make me feel like an alien, like this isn't my place and never will be. Jimmy still insists on walking into the village though. Told me to ignore it, to get out of the car and walk with him. I couldn't. So I drive everywhere and he walks. Though he complains that walking here's isolating, eyes on you, not a word spoken. You talk about the beautiful country lanes to walk out here, Jimmy wouldn't know about that. I wouldn't.

> *(Beat.)*

MATTY. Why didn't yer say somethin' to 'em?

OLIVIA. Seen my Babamukuru George be stared at in the street, not a word said, just eyes following him. Seen a stranger tell him to go back to the ghetto. Seen his surname mangled hopelessly. I mean how hard is George Dudzai to say if you just ask how to say it? Sometimes it was even, an anxious smile and then, 'I'm not even going to try and say that, can I call you George?' And he never said a thing. Thing is neither did I. No one cared what he thought. No one cares what I think.

MATTY. Old George? *(The unfamiliarity is tough, but he is determined.)* Ba-ba-mu-ku-ru George. Didn't realise.

OLIVIA. *(Laughs a little, pleased at **MATTY**'s sincere attempt.)* Why would you? Not happening to you.

MATTY. Always thought this village was...the people here... we didn't do things like that.

OLIVIA. Most people like to think they're only good. Don't like being told some things they do might not be.

> *(Beat.)*

MATTY. I care what yer think.

> *(**OLIVIA** smiles at him.)*
>
> *(A moment.)*
>
> *(**MATTY** takes out his final Mars Celebration.)*

Go on it's my last one.

> *(**OLIVIA** takes it, breaks it in half and holds out half to him.)*

(Accepting the portion of chocolate.) Cheers.

> *(**MATTY** devours his, while **OLIVIA** has a brief hesitation before she eats hers. Both **OLIVIA** and **MATTY** eat their chocolate together.)*
>
> *(Time passes as **OLIVIA** and **MATTY** search for insects for the female curlew. Time has passed. It is 4:40 a.m. on the Twenty-first of June. Midsummer's Day. The full Shropshire dawn chorus begins, quietly at first and gradually louder and louder. The sounds of the dawn chorus at Lake Chivero are also mixed in. Light is coming into the early morning sky rapidly. Full sunrise happens by the end of the play.)*

> (**OLIVIA** *stands contemplating the dark rooms of Jacaranda farmhouse.*)

MATTY. *(To the curlew.)* Our girl's lookin' better.

> (**OLIVIA** *glances down at the curlew and notices something.*)

OLIVIA. Hey, what's that? It looks like, no, can't be.

MATTY. *(Rushing to the angle* **OLIVIA** *is at.)* What yer goin' on about? (**MATTY***'s amazed.*) Don't believe it.

OLIVIA. I'm not seeing things?

MATTY. Yer beauty!

OLIVIA. Shhh! Shhh. It's hatching.

> (**OLIVIA** *looks down at the baby curlew chick that's hatching. She claps her hand over her mouth and is overcome with emotion.*)
>
> (*As the chick clumsily struggles out from under his mother, not yet used to his large feet,* **OLIVIA** *grabs* **MATTY***'s hand.*)
>
> (*Through the following, the curlew chick sits under his mother's wing, and she nuzzles and cleans his feathers with her beak.*)

Matty look. He's perfect.

MATTY. *(Indicating the curlew.)* Nice one girl.

> (*They both stare at the curlew chick with pure and utter joy.*)
>
> (**OLIVIA** *suddenly turns to* **MATTY***.*)

OLIVIA. *(Handing* **MATTY** *her box of sleeping pills.)* Hold on to these for me?

*(**MATTY** puts the box in a pocket of his combat trousers.)*

(Impulsive.) Call him.

MATTY. It's early; he'll be asleep.

OLIVIA. He'll want to hear from you.

MATTY. Not sure.

OLIVIA. If I was him I'd want to hear from you.

*(**MATTY** looks across the field to the dark Jacaranda farmhouse.)*

MATTY. I will if you will.

OLIVIA. He's been up all night.

MATTY. So've you. If I was him I'd want to hear from yer.

*(The sound of the female elephant trumpeting mutedly is heard. **OLIVIA** looks out into the audience in the direction of the sound. **MATTY** does too.)*

What is that?

OLIVIA. *(Amazed and a little confused.)* You can hear it?

(The elephant trumpets again. More confidently this time.)

MATTY. *(Squinting in the direction of the elephant call.)* That's impossible!

OLIVIA. *(Laughs with joy as she speaks.)* I hear it. Call him now. Trust me.

*(**MATTY** looks at **OLIVIA** as if she's lost her mind.)*

(Beat.)

(He calls anyway.)

*(**OLIVIA** and **MATTY** each hold their mobiles to their ears and call Jimmy and Ste respectively.)*

*(Lots of jacaranda flowers cascade down over everything. **MATTY** sees them for the first time and marvels at this seeming miracle. **OLIVIA** reacts to them too.)*

OLIVIA. Jimmy?

MATTY. Ste?

(The sound of the curlew chick calling is heard. His mother joins him.)

*(Lights down as **MATTY** and **OLIVIA** turn, phones still to their ears, and look out into the audience and into the brilliantly sun-filled morning sky.)*

(The female elephant trumpets loudly.)

The End